The Narc Survival Guide

Published by Melissa Shim

Imprint: Lulu.com

Copyright 2022 by Melissa Shim

Cover Design: Melissa Shim

Author and Editor: Melissa Shim

ISBN: 978-1-4583-8387-7

ABOUT THE AUTHOR

After many years of domestic abuse from my prior marriage, I developed a mindset knowing I had to get out of my situation. I knew I was better than I was being treated and I deserved much more than I was receiving. My values, morals, and ethics far exceeded those of my abuser.

I was full of anger, loneliness, and was very scared. My self-esteem and lack of confidence were destroyed. I had no identity. Everything I had been told by my abuser, I believed and nothing I was being told was the truth. Yet, in the back of my mind, I still had it in me to find myself again.

It was my turn and my time to find something I had not had much of…..happiness. This whole time I had been letting other people define who I was. I let other people control my happiness. When indeed, I learned that only I had the power and control to make myself happy and not let others choose my happiness for me. Happiness is truly a masterpiece after one has learned to master peace.

After many years of domestic abuse in my prior marriage, I developed a mindset knowing I had to get out of my situation. I knew I was better than I was being treated and I deserved much more than I was receiving. My values, morals, and ethics far exceeded those of my abuser. So, I set out to find myself and give myself a personal identity or brand. It was not easy, but it was so worth it. Even today I am still practicing self love. There is always something more to be learned, to be read, to be heard, and to experience.

I hope this book will help you with your cause as much as it helps me to write about them.

Melissa Shim

My message to you…

Narcissism does not discriminate. It will break your heart and tear you apart. And when your heart is lost, the narcissist will make you lose your mind.

After being beaten down so much, you start to believe in everything but yourself. And if that's not enough for the narcissist to have fun with, they will start to mess with your kids and your family to keep you in their control.

It's a terrible position to be in, but you can escape!

Never lose sight of yourself, what you are capable of doing, and what you stand for. There is hope.

I am living proof of that and there are many others that took the same path as I to escape the control of their abuser.

Sending positive vibes your way. Be strong and don't look back!

Melissa Shim

CHAPTER 1

THE EXTERNAL SIGNS OF A NARCISSIST

The purpose of this chapter is to add to your understanding of narcissism if you are already familiar with it. Hopefully, this will help you pick up on red flags which is part of their everyday natural behavior. I want you to learn and discern what is right and appropriate for you in relationships. Below you can find 10 red flags that are external signs of a narcissist and how to identify them.

The primary ingredients of narcissism are high control, low empathy needs for superiority, an attitude of entitlement, and manipulative and exploitive ways of dealing with people. Perhaps you know someone like this but didn't realize it. I had heard of the term narcissism but really didn't know much about it. That is until I married one. Again, I did not know what he was, as the person I was getting to know was totally different from the person he actually was. And keep in mind, I speak of a male here, narcissism takes place in any gender, home, lifestyle, etc...

Once you learn more about the external signs of a narcissist, you will begin to see there are more than you think. However, we should not confuse narcissism with someone just being a jerk or having an ego.

I am very passionate about this subject as I was once married to a narcissist and it was the worst years of my life. It still continues even after divorce as my kids are subjected to the very same thing. I have put many hours into researching narcissism to find the best way to co-parent with one. Everything I read told me to cut all ties. But, I could not due to my children. So many more hours went into researching and trying to understand what makes a narcissist tick. Eventually, I found ways to make my life better and more bearable while trying to co-parent.

So, let's move on......

10 External Signs Of A Narcissist

Criticism is common

The narcissist tends to be very critical. Sure we all have our moments we may criticize but the narcissist does it quite often. They complain about someone, an event, how things did not measure up, you get it. They do this frequently to the point that you get the impression nothing can make them happy or please them. And it is true as the narcissist has to be superior. They like finding things that illustrate to them that people and events are inferior to them.

They tend not to delve too deep into your emotions

Let's start with an example. Perhaps you went to a party with family and friends you do not see often. You express to the narcissist that you really enjoyed your time with them at the party and it was very rewarding. Now, the normal person would say something to the effect of, "Yes, I can tell you had a good time. Tell me more about it." They ask penetrating questions so they can get to know you on a personal basis.

A narcissist does not care about that. They may say "Oh, that's nice." But, they do not show a lot of interest because you are not them. The only person they need to focus on is their own.

They hijack conversations

So, you are talking about an event or trying to make plans. The narcissist may say, "Yes, that reminds me of a time that I did something like that." They will go on and on about their experience. Then you sit there thinking, "I was about to tell you what my experience was." You then realize that they do not even care. Their favorite topic to talk about is themselves.

They lack reflective thinking

Narcissists can be intellectual. They can have all sorts of ideas about right from wrong and what is good and what is bad. They might be able to explain concepts and ideas really well. But they can not think reflectively.

If you are in a relationship and you are trying to discuss who we are or where we are going, it's tied to some meaning and purpose. For a narcissist, it is too much trouble and they want you to look to them to tell you what to do. They get bored rather quickly to go deeper and into the root of things unless they are the ones who get to call all of the shots. Then they can talk forever about that.

They can excuse any and every mistake or failure they make

If there was a failure. It was someone else's fault, not their own. For example: if they had problems in a relationship, they may talk about how moody that person was, or that their partner cheated on them, or they had other expectations. If it was a sporting event and their team lost, it was because of the referees. If a business venture or organization didn't go well then someone else is at fault for that. The excuses are endless.

They do not like saying they made a mistake or that they have totally blown it. Hell, they can't even say they say they are sorry to anyone. A narcissist cannot express negativity of any sort about themselves because to them, that means they are vulnerable and they are no longer in the superior position. That really scares a narcissist.

They have a lot of expectations for you, an agenda

The narcissist has an agenda for everyone, They have a lot of expectations for you and everyone they encounter in general. A narcissist will use words like must, have to, had better, got to, should, supposed to, etc. They use these words, as they believe there is an agenda to unfold and it happens to coincide with the way the narcissist is thinking. The narcissist insists things have to play out in line with their agenda. They do not allow for nuances. Narcissists are very black and white with no room to move in their thought processes.

Conflicts are not managed successfully (very common flag)

If you get into a conflict with a narcissist, you may think it is a conflict but the narcissist will think it's a contest. Who is correct and who is incorrect. Do you want to guess who the incorrect person will be? Not the narcissist. They will shame, blame and overwhelm you to prove their point. If they do not get what they want, they move on to the passive aggressive way. They will shut down, not return calls, texts, or what have you. If you are in conflict with a narcissist, they will see you as the loser and they will let everyone know about it too.

There is no spirit of teamwork.

A healthy person would compromise and ask to hear each side. Each person will share their needs, feelings, and thoughts. They work it out.

They exaggerate their own positives while minimizing their own negatives

For example, their kids are doing well in school, but when the narcissist speaks, their kids are the best in their class. Or at age 48, they still talk about a play they allegedly made in high school. They may talk about the things that went well, but they do not like to talk about the things that may have gone bad. As a result, you do not get a real feeling of intimacy, Nor do they seem to be human. As we all make mistakes and should be able to talk about them and learn from them.

They love to learn the negatives about you because that gives them power over you. But you will never know their own negatives.

They can be very impressed with the external signs of success

A narcissist will like living in a bigger house, driving a better car, dressing in the finest clothes, and hanging around those who they think "matter" the most. They want to be noticed for their bling, success and being around those in decision making positions. They cannot accept being just average, plain or normal, To a narcissist, that is not very appealing.

There is a general sense of close-mindedness

The narcissist does not like hearing from other people. They become very impatient with people because they do not want to slow down to hear someone else's thoughts or feelings or needs. A narcissist thinks, "If the world would think like me, we would all be better off." They do not want to be bothered by listening to someone else's thoughts and interpretations. They expect you to do what they want you to do.

Questions to ask yourself before moving on with a narcissist

Am I being asked to be loyal to someone who does not want to reciprocate loyalty toward me?

Do I sense that this person will ultimately have a low opinion of me? In particular, when my humanity shows up. (Always go with your gut feelings)

Is this someone I can be safe with when difficulties arise? This would include relationships, business, parenting, etc....

Do I get the feeling there are certain things I do not know or they do not want me to know about them?

Learn how to read these red flags or external signs of a narcissist and tie them back to some of the primary characteristics of narcissism (control, low empathy, etc...) You will begin to be able to read people better the more you look for these external signs of a narcissist and understand them. As usual, go with your gut feeling. And do not forget to ask yourself the questions listed above. The bottom line is, narcissists do not think like most people do, in a general manner. If something feels off, it most likely is.

Chapter 2

7 TYPES OF ABUSIVE NARCISSIST

After reading this chapter you will learn about the abusive narcissists and the 7 types to avoid.

Narcissism, like anything else, has several categories. Of course, the typical narcissist has common characteristics such as being grandiose, self-infatuated, self-centered, arrogant, excessive need for admiration, lacking empathy, manipulative, patronizing and demanding. Whew......just to name a few......lol. However, we will dive into the different types of narcissism to gain better insight as to how to recognize one.

As you read this chapter, I want to warn you that I write this book on narcissism as I lived through more than 20 years of daily abuse and the abuse even continues after leaving the situation. This book is not to lecture you or ridicule you, but only to make you aware so you do not make the same mistake I did. It was a horrible experience! So please keep an open mind and read carefully.

Vanity/Static Narcissist

The look of external success can be very misleading! From abusive narcissists' thoughts, they are thinking I have arrived, I am the most important person here, I am successful. all while lacking tons of confidence. They are very attention-seeking while wearing the finest clothes and accessories and driving high-end cars. Oh, and it does not stop there. The vanity narcissist has to hang out with the "right" people (usually those that validate them). They are all about impressions via appearance. If the narcissist feels you are "lesser" to them, they will be very condescending and snob-like towards you. Being superficial is their specialty.

I have to laugh because if there was one thing my ex was not, he certainly was not the vanity narcissist. But he did care about impressions and tried to hang out with elites.

The Entitled Narcissist

These parties may or may not have the notion to look successful as the vanity narcissist, but they do need to be unique and different. There are no boundaries for them. They still think they are above you, but they all think they are above all else too. They do not believe in the norm of regulations and rules. As far as they are concerned, rules do not apply to them. They think they are "different" and should be treated that way as well.

These types of abusive narcissists will also refuse to do menial tasks. Again, they think they are better than that and these tasks are beneath them. On the other hand, they do believe you should be doing tasks for them, but they will never reciprocate unless there is something in it for them.

When called out, they feel it is an insult. As if you "don't know who they are." You know, they are Hollywood status and should be treated as such. They feel the world owes them and you should be "thankful" to be a part of their life.

They are always in search of favored treatment. No matter how much my ex abused myself, he was always the victim.

I do not make this shit up. The one I was married to was so entitled

The Malignant Narcissist

My ex had this characteristic about him too. These abusive narcissists are very destructive in nature. They will tear others down and mess with them emotionally and mentally all while trying to maintain control over their victim.

This type of narcissist is very cold, calculating and very uncaring. They do not care about the impact they have on others. In my situation, he was even evil towards his kids. Oftentimes, if the narcissist sees you hurting, this fuels their fire to continue with the abuse. It almost seems as if they enjoy hurting others.

They have no empathy, hence no appreciation or feelings towards others who may struggle or be hurting due to their own behaviors.

It's their way or no way!

I know this stuff is hard to believe because the normal person does not think this way, but believe me, it is real. I have tons of horror stories I lived and will maybe one day share.

The Covert Narcissist

This group tends not to be super flashy or stand out at first. They fly below the radar. At first, they appear to be normal, but watch out! This was the trap that initially pulled me into my relationship with the abusive narcissist that I unfortunately attracted. As time passed I found out he wanted nothing to do with accountability. He was very unreliable. They are very secretive, and when it is too late. you find out that you do not know this person at all.

When I look back at my 13 years of marriage., it was all a lie. Not a bit of it was true, And if it was, I will never know what was the truth and what was not.

They are super passive/aggressive! One moment they may show signs of anger, But be aware, they are not done until they silently punish you. For someone who wants dominance, they do it with stubbornness in a very child-like way. Such as a toddler throwing a tantrum and then going into the silent treatment.

If they do not agree with you on something, they will hold grudges. And again, they don't stop there. Afterward, there is no forgiveness or forgetfulness. Sooner or later they will find revenge.

There is no sense of humor with these types of abusive narcissists. They are serious if you cross them in their own mind.

The Victim Narcissist

Yup, I said it earlier and here it is again. These abusive narcissists are extremely manipulative in what seems like a helpless fashion. They delegate and find others who will sympathize with them in order to get them to do things for them.

The person I had married would make his own family feel sorry for him in order to get them to do things for them. They have people believing they are really having a rough time and then these good people help out, thinking they are helping him. When in all actuality, he is using them to get things done. And the narcissist then starts to think, "What are they going to do for me next?" When you serve them, they see you as a servant beneath them.

If you stick around long enough, you will see that helping them out never seems to make things any better for them. Before you know it, they are out playing the victim again. The acts of service, words of affirmation, etc….it's never enough for the narcissist. It is impossible to satisfy them. Once you give them something, they expect it the next time. And more is never good enough for them.

The Know-It-All Narcissist

This type of narcissist feels they need no guidance or direction from anyone at all. Even if they are wrong, they are going to tell you how to do things. On the flip side, they are very terrible at listening if they even listen at all.

When talking to this type of narcissist, it's like talking to a wall. They will be so stubborn and argument with just about anything.

Here is a shocker, they have a high opinion of themselves. They are very competitive. Everything is a game to them and they love to win!

The know-it-all narcissist has to one-up everyone to look good and in their own mind, keep everyone in check. Because remember, we cannot function without them. The bottom line is they are always right.

The Control Freak Narcissist

They are at the mercy of being a perfectionist and things need to be exactly the way they want. If you deviate from their thoughts at all, even though you may be right and they are wrong, all hell will break loose.

These abusive narcissists will be very critical and obnoxiously bossy. Keep in mind, nothing you do will be good enough for them. Nothing at all. Think about the control freak that does not have narcissistic traits and then add to that someone who cares about nothing but themselves. This is your control freak narcissist.

"Defensive" is a word to describe the control freak narcissist., especially when things are not going their way. If you try to rationalize with them or have any type of difference against them, they become very defensive because they see this as a personal attack. Not just a difference of opinion, as most people would see it.

Since they feel the need to be in control, you need to do things their way. They have no empathy for the way you feel and you will not change their minds to even compromise with you. They do not care how you feel, nor will they take the time to even consider how you might feel.

Common Theme of Any Narcissist

Under no circumstances are you allowed to be yourself!

Your primary job is to focus and cater to the narcissist. They want to take away from you who you really are. They will manipulate and mold you in any way they can. **DO NOT LET THEM DO THIS. ALWAYS BE TRUE TO YOURSELF!!!**

To conclude, you now have been warned! These are the 7 types of narcissists to avoid at all costs. None of them will benefit you no matter how much money, charm, fame, brains or what have you they lead you to bring to the table. The horror I lived with portrayed all of the types of narcissism except for the vanity narcissist. Once you get to know one though, they are all pretty much the same in their own way.

Chapter 3

REASONS THEY ATTRACT AND UNDERSTAND HOW

After reading this chapter you will be more aware of the narcissist, reasons they attract and how to understand them. Narcissists are some of the worst people to know, be in a relationship with, or have to work with.

They come in the form of co-workers, parents, significant others, friends and more. When around a narcissist, it can lead to very unhealthy relationships and leave you in a very vulnerable and mentally unstable mindset.

This chapter is my story and will hopefully make you more aware of the narcissist, the reasons they attract, and how to understand them. Hopefully, you will not fall into the same trap as I once did.

So, just to make you aware, I had heard of the term narcissist and knew what the term meant. However, to deal with one or be around one, I had no clue how to identify. Matter of fact, I had married one and did not even know it. That is, until 13 years later when I figured it out.

Now keep in mind, I was a college-educated woman with many friends. I treated people with respect and I was well-liked by all. I had always surrounded myself with positive people and was very caring especially of those close to me.

Then I met my match. And, because I could never think like him, I was usually blindsided by things. It wasn't until during my divorce that I researched the shit out of narcissism. And I knew then it was going to be a tough battle.

The daily question I asked myself was "What in the hell was I thinking?" And yes, those close to me were thinking and asking the same thing. To this day I still question it, but I figured out why I married him.

Do you want to know?

I did not marry the guy he actually was hiding behind the mask. I married the fictitious character he led myself and everyone else to believe he was. To this day he still has his followers (who have no confidence and self-esteem themselves) or his "flying monkeys." There will be more to come on that topic.

The Narcissist, Reasons They Attract

Awareness happens after the fact

As I had noted in the paragraphs prior, I was not aware, because I did not know what was going on. You don't; think like a narcissist, so your brain is not wired to think that way. The normal person would not know what was going on. The normal person does not sit and think about how they are going to exploit people or manipulate others. The narcissist is always thinking of ways to dominate and intimidate others to keep in their mind....superiority.

You may be there by default

Perhaps you may have had a parent who was a narcissist, or you may work with one. For family members, you may grow up thinking it is the norm. If you work with one you may not be able to totally ignore it. As for me, I just showed up. I did not ask to be put in that position.

In my case, I had known this person before but they were not pursuing me. I had no interest anyway so it was not a focus for me. When we were married, it was too late. I did not see the red flags until after much time had been invested in the relationship. And then there were children. Ugh! If I had known then, I never would have reproduced with such a poor example of life. Because now, my children are enduring the same thing.

Narcissists tend to be quite the charmers

I fell for this one hook, line, sinker! In normal relationships, the parties try to impress and engage to learn more about the other to see if this is something they want to pursue or not. Your goal is to find common ground with each other.

The narcissist charms for different reasons. Their intent is to manipulate and exploit you and those close to you, including their own children. The narcissist will say nice things to you, take you on trips and buy things for you so you will find them flattering. But, trust me, that all changes.

If it is too good to be true, go with your gut feeling, it most likely is not even close to what you think.

From an emotional standpoint, they make you feel loved, wanted and appreciated. The narcissist is a good reader of people. I have found they usually feed on vulnerable or weak people. Now, I will admit, when I started dating my ex, I was pretty down due to another event. My abuser knew exactly what I needed at that time. No joke, I was easily won with charm and a caring demeanor.

I say this because I watched him feed on someone else after were divorced. It was then that I could pretty much predict his next steps. Luckily for the woman he was dating, she figured out who he really was.

They really pour on the charm quickly and love-bomb you. Because they have to get you drawn in quickly or you might figure out their master plan.

Do you like being a caregiver?

You are the one who wears their heart on their sleeve. You are the loving one who gets gratification for caring for others. In a healthy world, those are great traits to have. But when you are caught up in a relationship with a narcissist, this will be hazardous.

The key for the caregiver is that the one you are caring for appreciates and reciprocates. Again, you will not get this from the narcissist.

The narcissist will take advantage of your services and let those skills of yours grow deeper until they can turn them on you. This is yet another example of "you don't know what you don't know." It's not the norm.

You may have been in a place of emotional need

As I have told you, the narcissist reads people very well. They have to so that their disguise is not blown and they are always superior to you. The narcissist knows this and that is when the charm kicks in. They see your vulnerability and lack of confidence and self doubt.

You are fed with things you want to hear and the narcissist is well aware of your need for that.

The narcissist is looking for someone they can dominate. You don't think that way, but they are. Again, "you don't know what you don't know."

The narcissist offers a lot of fun and pleasure

Similar to the charm they overwhelm you with, they will give you things you never had or do things with you that you have never done. I was flattered with trips and hiking, repelling, scuba diving and all of those things I had never done but wanted to. As usual, that ended very soon after. The endgame was the total opposite. It's all a facade.

The narcissist is not as dysfunctional in the early stages

It may take a life event to change how quickly the narcissist changes. For example, everything may be going their way. They have you, they got a promotion, people are starting to notice them more. This may cause the ego to grow even faster and bigger. It feeds the need for superiority! Superiority is the fuel for a narcissist. This is usually due to their own insecurities.

On the flip side, it could be the opposite. The narcissist may have been disappointed many times throughout life and as they age, they have a mindset that no one else is going to make them feel that way again. They feel angry and have a power and control mindset.

Things to remember

When anyone comes at you with a lot of persuasions, be very patient and cautious with them and the situation. Persuasion is a sign of control and that is the narcissist's ultimate goal!

Consider who you are and what you want. As noted above, do not fall into the persuasion tactic they are playing.

Stay away from the narcissist's "All or nothing" way of thinking. They will use dominance and to you, it will all seem black and white. This is when the mental and verbal abuse starts. They will tell you how much of a terrible person you are and more. They bring you up and then tear you down, bring you up and then tear you down again. It's not only disgusting one could do this to another person, but it is very vicious too. It's their intent, which makes it worse.

After you leave this situation, go back to your own personal basics. (This is huge.!) After 13 years of mental and verbal abuse, I felt like I had no identity. I did not know who I was. But little did my abuser know, I would prevail and now I am stronger than ever! It was a long process but well worth it! Find your core values and morals.

Carefully consider the input from other people. You might even go as far as soliciting input from other people. I failed miserably at this. People would often tell me that he did not treat others very nicely or he did not respect others, talked poorly about others. So what did I do? I made excuses for him. Listen to others. They are outsiders looking in.

Practice assertiveness. listen carefully and try to read them cautiously. Do not let them control you and dominate you. You deserve the same respect you gave them. Be clear and stand firmly as to who you are. Don't back down or change your morals and values.

You should now know a little bit more about the narcissist, reasons they attract and how to understand them. The takeaway from all of this is to know who you are and what you want. Do not deviate from that without first considering over time. Don't settle just because.

Chapter 4

THE MIND GAMES OF A NARCISSIST

After reading this chapter, you will be more alert and able to pick up on the mind games played by the narcissist. Narcissists are very manipulative and controlling. They use your own mind to do both. This is a warning of the mind games of a narcissist, so know them now! Don't be part of the narcissistic supply.

Be aware that the narcissist NEVER takes responsibility for their own actions. They will only blame you. So to rationalize with them is impossible unless they have an underlying agenda that will benefit them in the end. Hence, the importance of learning and recognizing the mind games that are played on you.

While reading these mind games, think about how you need to react so you do not find yourself playing along and falling into the trap.

Mind Games: 1

I Want You To Trust Me

They will act extremely friendly with you.

The narcissist will seem like they are interested in you. Let me tell you now, they are not. They will ask you questions about yourself and not give back the same courtesy, And in the long term, they will use your answers against you in some form or fashion eventually. You just won't know it when they do.

Due to their curiosity, they may even entice you to open up. The narcissist will feed on your vulnerability. They will get you to open up because they can be so easy to talk to. But this is all part of their plan. That is great in a healthy relationship but with a narcissist, their end game is not so nice. And again, they will not open up to you. They will figure out what your needs are and what makes you hurt, only to be turned against you in the future.

Mind Games: 2

They Begin To Develop An Upper Hand Over You

Once you start to trust them and believe in them, all of a sudden they will start to criticize you. EX: You should not have done it that way, or Why did you do that? Then they will go into I am right and you need to do it this way. Or I am better than you, watch how I do it. Something to those effects. Remember from my past posts, the narcissist thinks they are smarter than you and are superior to you.

The narcissist is very self-confident and has an inflated amount of correctness and confidence both. They will tell you you are wrong and that they are right. They will lead you to believe that you just need to do what they say. Again, the narcissist honestly does believe they are smarter than you.

Mind Games: 3

They Will Instill Fear Into You

It feeds their narcissistic supply when you fear them. This is very intentional! The fear may be through their judgment, stubbornness or perhaps they show strong emotions.

You will start to second guess yourself and fear that you need to do what they tell you to do. It's mentally taxing to deal with all of the mental stress that goes along with the fear itself. Also, a part of their plan. Please be aware that this can happen to the most confident people. Narcissism does not discriminate.

If you try to show you are right or unique, etc....this will cause you problems. This is the very thing that causes fear. You cannot be yourself because you have mentally trained that whatever you do is never going to be good enough.

Mind Games: 4

They Will Sabotage You and Your Credibility and Competency Behind Your Back

They will isolate you from those who know you and like you, including your own family and children if you have them. My ex did this to me. I was doing everything for the kids, working full time and trying to maintain a household. All the while he was out coaching hockey and things like that. I had no identity for years. Little did I know this was him controlling me mentally.

The narcissist will talk behind your back to those that are close to you. For example, you may receive a compliment from your best friend, but the narcissist will find the opportunity to take your best friend aside and tell them things that will make them question you. The criticism will start. You can only hope that the people they are talking to see right through their bullshit. But not everyone will. I quickly found out who my loyal friends were and who his followers and flying monkeys were.

When the narcissist has others thinking you are not competent, this keeps the narcissist in the "superior seat!" They see others will start to look down on you as well. This too feeds the narcissist's supply.

Mind Games: 5

The Narcissist Will Find Out Your Flaws And Then Use Them Against You

The narcissist has a very good memory when it comes to remembering your flaws (even if they are not real). We all have them, right? No, wrong. The narcissist, if you ask them, is darn near perfect. When you open up to them and share f some times you failed or made mistakes. they will hold onto those moments and use them against you later to criticize you when you are awarded accolades of some sort or someone may praise or compliment you. If the narcissist even sees a sign that you have an ounce of confidence, they will tear you down with your own experiences. I also stated they will remind you of something that may not have even happened. The narcissist is known for telling half-truths and then you have to find out what is true and what is not if any of it is even true at all.

When they ask you questions to learn more about you, it is not because they are interested. It is because they are collecting data. So keep in mind, if you share, make sure they share back. Don't have a one-sided conversation. It will cost you later.

And if you are looking for forgiveness from them….hell-to-the-no. They will not do that. They will use that situation over and over.

Mind Games: 6

They Are The Victim In Almost Any Situation

They will not accept blame or take responsibility for their own mistakes. And heaven forbid you to embarrass them by accident, such as accidentally spilling a drink on them or something so minor. If the narcissist messed up, it was because of someone else's error, not because of their own fault. They will throw someone under the bus, even if it is not true or warranted.

Mind Games: 7

They Make You Feel It Is Your Duty or Your Obligation

They will use phrases such as you must, you have to, you need to, etc. And when you refuse, they come at you harder. As noted before, this is very taxing and frustrating. It really messes with your mind and they wear you down so much.

They write the rules and the rules will benefit them and their agenda. It's their way or no way.

Key Notes:

Do not give them the reaction they want.

Keeping calm and mentally alert and stable is important.

There are reasonable times in which you can confront them. Set the boundaries they are so trying to control.

Don't get into arguments with a narcissist. You are wasting so much of your time and energy. You will never get your point across or have them see both sides of the argument.

The ultimate goal for the narcissist is for you to lose your uniqueness and your identity, or be who you really are. They will strip you down and mold your own mind into a way they can control you. The purpose of this article is to not let this happen to you. I have given you some identifiers to use to avoid the same mistake I did. Don't let them keep you in a state of confusion and doubt. And never let them or anyone else, take away who you are!

Chapter 5

GASLIGHTING

Gaslighting, is the manipulation happening to you? Are you aware of the signs to know if you are being manipulated by way of gaslighting? Do you know what gaslighting is? After reading this chapter you will have a better understanding of what gaslighting is, how it may be used against you, where it comes from, the signs to acknowledge it may be happening to you, and how to react to the manipulation. Do not let the abuser take away your identity and who you really are!

What Is Gaslighting?

Gaslighting is a tactic an abuser uses to gradually gain power and control over a victim. The narcissist is a major culprit to this kind of behavior. Gaslighting is an ongoing form of manipulation that causes one to doubt what they see, hear and or experience. At one point in my life, I was a victim of this sort of abuse for several years.

In fact, I was manipulated so badly, I was once a confident woman, who would now doubt my own perception of the world around me. Again, this method of mental abuse is used by toxic narcissists. It's a type of brainwashing that can cause one to lose your entire sense of self and identity. Repeatedly experiencing gaslighting will destroy your self worth and cause you to question reality at times. And after a while, the victim starts to rely on the abuser's mental stability, more than their own. This makes the victim feel they cannot leave their situation.

As a victim, you may hear the key phrases that are said to you time and time again: "I never said that. You are making things up again.", "I don't want to talk about this again.", "Are you sure? You know you have a bad memory.", or "Why are you so sensitive all of the time?" If you hear these phrases being said to you repetitively, please see them as red flags and do not doubt your own judgment!

Gaslighting takes place in the context of a relationship (could be work, family, friend or partner) in which one person is manipulative, self-centered, low on empathy, and has a vested interest in always being right. Does this sound familiar to you? Does this fit the definition of a narcissist? Yes, yes it does.

The end goal of the narcissist is to create a sense of confusion so that you then question who you are and how you interpret life.

So Where Does The Term Gaslighting Come From?

Loew's, Inc. Gaslight is a 1944 American psychological-thriller film, adapted from Patrick Hamilton's 1938 play Gas Light, about a woman whose husband slowly manipulates her into believing that she is going insane. You might check it out to get some visual and audio examples. I am not sure if I am at a point in life that I can watch it and not get angry since it did happen to me. Therefore, I cannot say if it is a good movie or not, but it does go to show the term has been around for a while.

Signs To Acknowledge

The gaslighter is not an honest person

The gaslighter is never honest about who they really are as a person. You have to remember, the narcissist has the mindset and believes they pretty much do everything right or correctly. This means all of the time. They are NEVER wrong (at least in their own minds). They exaggerate who they think they are as a person so you will never know their weaknesses, fears, vulnerabilities, etc. You are more prone to hear of their successes (whether true or not), versus any of their flaws. Last time I checked, we are all flawed individuals. When they assess who they are in a dishonest fashion, they will do the same to you.

The gaslighter is always looking for ways to find your flaws

They may do this through direct criticism. My abuser used this a lot on me. I could not do anything right in his eyes. I was told how rude I was and how I was not able to make sound decisions. This totally floored me as I was known as anything but rude to people. As far as decision making, it's what I do for a living in a fast-paced environment for hours every day. Yet, I was convinced after hearing time after time.

To support the narcissist's false data, they will be sure to let you know other people's interpretation of you, through the words and thoughts of a narcissist. For example, The narcissist may say: "I was talking to your mom last week. She does not want you to know, but she thinks you are crazy too." This happened to me a lot!. I was convinced my family had given up on me. My abuser was playing me against my family and friends and vice versa. It was so mentally frustrating, depressing, and exhausting to hear those things. Yet, I believed him over them, instead of asking my family and friends if this was truly what they said. But the gaslighter is going to let you know that people do not think highly of you.

You could be having a conversation with someone at a ball game or another event of some sort and the narcissist will tell you that you were being rude and hurting the person's feelings that you were talking to. You did not feel that you had a bad conversation. Matter of fact, you felt the conversation went well. However, after the gaslighter tells you how insensitive you were, you believe it. They leave you feeling doubtful.

The gaslighter will tell you how to interpret yourself

They will tell you how disrespectful you are when interacting with others. You do not feel you are, but they lead you to believe you are hurting others.

The gaslighter may insist your behavior is not appropriate towards others even if you disagree. Then they will proceed to let you know how wrong you are and attempt to support it again, with false statements from others. They try to smear your character or you as you know you.

The more you hear this, the more you start to believe it is true. This is what the narcissist wants to happen.

Now, let's flip the scenario and you start to attack the narcissist with their flaws and how critical and inconsiderate they are of you and your feelings. The narcissist will let you know that you misunderstood them or that you were not listening to them, etc. The TRUE victim will always be to blame. However, the narcissist in their mind is always the victim.

The gaslighter will talk about you behind your back

This one really frustrates me from one point but also is an eye-opener to another. My abuser did this all of the time and still continues today. He would talk poorly about me behind my back to my friends and family. There are really people out there who will listen to only one side of a story and make their own conclusions with just that one person's version. These are the people I learned to stay away from. They were the narcissist's "flying monkeys." On the other hand, I learned who my real friends were and who knew the person I really was, not who my abuser portrayed me to be. To this day, he has followers, but I see how ignorant they really are. I stay away from them.

I was portrayed as being mean to people and having a bad temper. My then spouse would tell people this behind my back. Who does this? In a normal relationship the spouse, if this were at all true, would be trying to help you, not put you down to others, let alone behind your back. But they say these things to others that are weak too and will most likely believe them. Stronger people know that what the narcissist says is not in line with your behavior towards them and who they see you as a person.

They repeat your criticisms over and over

The victim will try to compromise and discuss their concerns to the gaslighter, but the gaslighter will continue to argue with them and not even acknowledge their points or concerns. They will only tear you down even more. It's such a helpless and defeating position to be in.

The victim then starts to feel they cannot say anything or it will be used against them. They feel like they are targeted with characteristics that are not consistent with their true behavior. A sense of loneliness occurs because they are being talked about behind their backs. It really takes a negative mental toll on one's ability to think, sleep and function.

How To Respond To The Gaslighter

Everything is a game to the narcissist

Their game playing method makes you very angry and agitated. They want you to make yourself look like a fool to others and they do all of this behind closed doors. They win and will feed off of the anger and agitation they cause you. When they see this happening, they will use this method even more.

Do not waste your time and effort to get the narcissist to see your way. It is never going to happen. Doing so will only anger and agitate you more. I learned this the hard way, but I finally learned it. Do not engage with them when it comes to reasoning or understanding. When I learned this, things seemed to cool down because I would not respond. End the game with no response.

Focus on you

Redefine who you really are and focus on you. Find your lost identity and run with it. You define yourself. Do not let others!

If the narcissist has you believing you need to seek therapy, you are mean, you do not listen, etc. think about it. Do you need therapy? If so, get it. Are you mean? No, so check that off and don't focus on that. Only you have the final say as to who you are. No one else can take that away from you unless you let them. When evaluating yourself, be fair to yourself and do not be so harsh on yourself. We are our own worst critics.

Do not hand over your life to a narcissist who is actually the one who is not healthy or mentally stable.

Maintain control of your own core values and morals with confidence.

Make sure you keep good company. By that, I mean to surround yourself with others who understand you and are like you. There are many good people out there who want to surround themselves with the same. Stay out of the negative environments. Find those that appreciate you! Have courage, be vulnerable, and take risks with positive people.

To conclude, learn the signs of gaslighting. You will be better prepared to make the right choices for your own personal and mental health. Share with others so that they do not make the same mistakes I once made. Remember to be true to yourself and never sell yourself short.

Chapter 6

HOW TO TRAIN A NARCISSIST

How to train a narcissist in 3 clear, but not so easy steps. Sounds appealing right? After all, the narcissist spends years grooming you and manipulating you into someone you no longer know and takes away your identity. I think it is only appropriate that our abusers receive the same courtesy from us. Wouldn't you agree? So let's dive into how to train a narcissist in 3 clear, but not so easy steps.

How To Train A Narcissist

Step #1: Absolutely No Contact

I have researched and researched and researched the crap out of narcissism, narcissistic traits, indicators and how to control situations when engaged with a narcissist. Almost every article or book I have read advises you to absolutely cut off all contact with that party. I would agree.

So yes, the first step is easy for some to do and that is to cut off all ties to and with the narcissist.

But what happens when you have a child with a narcissist, or you have to work with a narcissist? You do not always have a viable choice as to if you can cut off all contact.

With kids you still have milestones, birthdays, holidays, graduations, weddings, etcetera might have to make some sort of contact with the narcissist.

As for the work environment, it's part of the job. You have to communicate with that person and work with that person to the point of getting the job done.

I had two children with a narcissistic husband and guess what? There was no way to cut off all ties. I still had to try and co-parent with this non-cooperative person.

So how do you do that?

You just do your best and keep your focus on the kids, not the situation between you and the narcissist. All too often, the kids get caught up in the nonsense.

Step #2: The Gray Rock Method

What is it?

So, how do we escape the child-like behavior of the narcissist without triggering their vindictive rage? "Gray Rock" is primarily a way of encouraging a narcissist to lose interest in you. So how does it differ from "no contact?" Glad you asked. With the Gray Rock Method you don't overtly try to avoid contact with the abuser. Instead, you allow contact but only give boring, monotonous responses so that they must go elsewhere for their supply of drama.

This took me forever to grasp. But once I did, dang did it made my life and stress level so maintainable! Not feeding into the narcissist's mind games, not only allowed me to remain in control of my own emotions and sanity and keep my composure, I was not feeling his nasty habit either. And, I remained in control of the situation.

It is very hard to do, but once I learned to filter through the criticism and only stick with facts, life was totally different.

When contact with you is consistently boring the mind of the narcissist is re-trained to expect boredom rather than drama. Narcissists are addicted to drama and they can't stand to be bored. It might even drive them to be crazier than they ever made you feel. Highly unlikely, but fun to think it's true.

With time, the narcissist finds a new victim to provide drama and then they will find themselves less drawn to you. Eventually, they just fade away. They may come and go depending on what is going on with the children, but the drama will be less. Mine actually happened pretty quickly once I figured it out.

Gray Rock is a way of training the narcissist to view you like a wall, a dull and emotionless wall — you bore them and they can't stand that kind of boredom and lack of drama. Stay positive and do not react! No negative reactions people! This is how they control you!

Why does it work

The narcissist needs constant stimulation to ward off their own boredom. Drama is a narcissist's remedy for boredom. In order for the drama to take place, the narcissist needs an audience and some players. Once the drama begins, they are provided an open buffet to a frenzy. The narcissist feels empowered and in complete control when pulling the strings that trigger our emotions. Any kind of emotion will do, as long as it is a response to their actions.

They are addicts. Their addiction to power is their main goal and priority. The power is acquired by way of our emotions. The narcissist needs to create drama so they can experience the power of manipulating our emotions.

As with any addiction, it is exhilarating to the narcissist when they get their supply of emotional responses. Like Pavlov's Dog, the more times the narcissist experiences a reward for their dramatic behavior, the more addicted they become. So, to reverse the poor behavior one needs to stop the reward. That is when the narcissist becomes furious with what is happening. If you stay the course and show no emotions, the narcissist will eventually decide that their toy is broken. It does not give them the same spitefulness and control as it once did

Step #3: Reward good behavior

Think about what the narcissist likes. They live for words of affirmation, love, attention and themselves placed on a pedestal. Even if it's in the form of love-bombing or idealization, that is way better than the alternative. Again, like Pavlov's Dog, reward good behavior. Now do not overdo it. Be sincere about it or they may see through your gestures.

Uh, yes, this step is pretty short. In my situation, there was not much good behavior to reward, but when there is, acknowledge it if you will.

Remember, narcissists rarely change their own behavior so you will need to accept this as your new way of life when dealing with them.

To conclude, you are now provided with three steps to train a narcissist. If you can do step number one and cut off all contact, that is your best route. However, if you are not that fortunate, there is still hope. Familiarize yourself with the Gray Rock Method and it will save you a lot of energy, mixed emotions, and more. Practice each time when dealing with the narcissist. It will get easier as you go and then again, your life will be so much simpler and you can rest knowing you now control their emotions. That is until they get bored with you and move on. The best end result you can accomplish!

Chapter 7

HEALTHY NARCISSISM - DID YOU KNOW?

Narcissism can have its benefits as it adds mental toughness. The personality trait can also lead to people feeling less stressed and being less vulnerable to depression than others. Healthy narcissism is real!

A narcissistic personality disorder is characterized by a person believing there are special reasons that make them different, better or more deserving than others.

They may feel upset if people do not recognize their apparent achievements, resent other people's successes and get upset if other people do not put their needs above their own.

The diagnosis of Narcissistic Personality Disorder is indeed very negative and includes characteristics such as arrogance, preoccupation with oneself, a need for constant admiration, and, most important, a lack of empathy for others.

But what if narcissism had a positive side? Guess what? It does!

Healthy narcissism can be related to self-worth and self-esteem, through self-love, but it is not exactly the same. It's taking pleasure in one's beauty, in the workings of one's mind, in the accomplishment of a tough job well done. It is great joy and satisfaction in oneself. It could range from a small victory such as scoring an A on a big test to a large accomplishment such as graduating with honors. Whatever the accomplishment, you are thoroughly in love with yourself for what you have achieved!

Narcissism In Childhood Development

Did you ever think of narcissism developing while in childhood? Think about it. Infants cry and what do we do? Feed them. They soil their pants. What do we do? We change them.

As they move on to toddlers, they take what they have learned and are familiar with them. They are very self-centered until they learn manners and how to be self- sufficient.

They learn words like "mine", "me", "I", and "no" to name a few. The world revolves around them and they have no regard for others. That is until they learn it. When they learn to be concerned for others, there becomes a balance between thinking of others, yet still have high self-esteem and self-confidence.

As one gets older, there is a greater appreciation of taking pleasure in oneself and one's impact on the world. This is healthy narcissism.

Are you seeing the pattern? It's taking some narcissistic traits but using them in a positive manner and still showing empathy and emotional intelligence.

What is The Importance of Healthy Narcissism?

If you can experience ecstatic joy in yourself, it will help you through difficult times.

So we go back to the beginning and where we started with healthy narcissism is less stress and less chance of depression. What if you worked at a job you did not like so much, but you need a job.

If you are able to apply narcissistic pleasure by creating your own achievable goals, it could get one through times of frustration and failure. Therefore, you just prevented burnout.

How about taking joy in one's beauty and positive impact on others. Do you see where the narcissistic approach can provide resilience during times of disappointment and heartbreak?

Do you see how this thought process can take away a lot of stress that could otherwise bring you down and spiral into depression?

Some people don't retain or develop healthy self-love from their childhoods. This can cause great damage to their adult years. How about an extremely self-centered parent demanding all of their child's attention, not leaving room for the child to revel in herself?

Does it feel wrong to accentuate and revel in your good qualities? Think about the concerns it brings to mind, such as fear of envy or "the evil eye"; or worries that you might be conceited. If this is the case for you, re-frame your healthy narcissism as gratitude for what you have been given. Being thankful for your natural talents may be a way to appreciate them without feeling too egotistical!

So fall in love with yourself and the qualities you bring to the world, all while sharing the same!

And remember... Think Me First! It's not selfish, it's necessary!

THANK YOU

It may come as a surprise to you, but you are the reason this book exists. It was built for you. Without you, I'd just be writing my thoughts into a journal somewhere.

But here you are. Your interest to learn is the best way to say "Thank You," and that encourages me to spend the time to put this tool together.

So, Thank You. You are much appreciated and you are worth it!

Melissa Shim

ADDITIONAL TOOLS

Blog: https://thinkmefirst.com

Facebook:
https://www.facebook.com/groups/thinkmefirst/

YouTube: https://tinyurl.com/thinkmefirst

Pinterest: https://www.pinterest.com/missythinkmefirst/

Rock Your Vibe Apparel:
https://rock-your-vibe.myspreadshop.com/